Wilderness

Poems By Tessie McCoy

ISBN: 1986921131
ISBN-13: 978-1986921138

This book is dedicated to my mother,

who always believed I could do anything.

Ma, I finally believe it too!

JOURNEY

PART I: ENTRY

1. Confession 2
2. Kamikaze 3
3. Mourning to Morning 5
4. Father's Day 7
5. Purposeless 10
6. Thoughts 11
7. Cracks in the Foundation 14
8. Murder At 53 15
9. Hurricane 17

PART II: LOST

1. '06 Rage 21
2. Run-On Reality 22
3. A Mess 24
4. Cover Up 25
5. Confusion 27
6. Associates 28
7. Single Epiphany 30
8. Reasons 31
9. Gone With the Wind 33
10. Weight Gain 34
11. The Live Experience 36
12. Who Am I 37
13. Love Name 39
14. Sunshine 41

PART III: SEARCHING

1. Second Epiphany 45
2. Tears From the Sky 46
3. Ready or Not 48
4. Hope 50

5. Funny Money 51
6. Ugly Beautiful 53
7. About Time 55
8. Love Undefined 56
9. 3a.m. Unclosed Thoughts 58
10. Prayer Poems 59
11. I Wonder 60
12. Queens & Kings 63
13. Self Discovery in America [Obama '08] 64
14. Journey to My Dream (After Kanye) 67
15. Relapse 69
16. March 3: Unequivocal 71
17. Direction 73
18. Dreaming to Wake Up 74

PART IV: HOME
1. Recalculating Route 81
2. War, Peace 82
3. Selfish Love 84
4. Alive 85
5. Forgiveness 86
6. Choose Freedom [4a.m. Revelation] 90
7. Love Defined [After Forgiveness & Freedom] 91
8. Today I Became A Bird 94
9. Something Really Joyful 96
10. The Banjo Lesson 97
11. Wilderness 100

An accurate depiction of my experiences then, to truthfully reflect my existence now…

Part I: Entry

Confession

Confession: I fall asleep without
wiping the tears from my face and
hope that someone will see them and
ask me what's wrong.

...No one ever does.

~~Kamikaze~~

Things look unstable here.
Where exactly is here?
This place, so hard to recognize
through the pupils of my eyes,
Objects are out of place.
Fires burning, smoke and ash fill
this crowded space.
There's no known order.
Everything's a mess.

Words flashing past like:
Clothes, mom, money, time,
love, future, self, why...

Eventually sentences are formed that
sound like:
If I had some money I'd buy
some clothes.
I really miss my mother.
Time is running out.
Nobody can make this decision
but you.
Who loves you?
I'm too young to go through
this...

My mind races through the maze of thoughts lost in my brain,
A forest full of pain,
A kamikaze.

But when that God filled wind blows through,
Placing everything back into its divine order
While clearing the smoke from the trees
Letting the spirit of the sun show through,
Maybe then I will finally know.
Maybe then I will finally grow.

Mourning to Morning

Didn't sleep much that night and I cried all morning.
And now 7 years later feels like I'm still in mourning.

See when you left you did it without warning.
Only a kiss and a hug, you left me with your love.
But over these 7 years that love hasn't been enough;
I no longer feel your arms around me from that last hug.
And I find myself asking for one more like it was a drug.

Like your love was a drug and you were my supplier
Supplying me with all that I could ever need or desire.
You gave me words when I didn't know what to say,
Fun when there was no one outside to play, and comfort.

Comfort when I thought no one would come for me.
Like the time I watched Candy Man and couldn't sleep,
Or the times when my brother used to constantly pick on me.

And that night you hugged, kissed me, and told me you loved me.
So how could you leave me?
Leave me when there was so much left for you to see,
So much left for us to do.
And now 7 years later,
Feels like I'll forever be mourning you...

~~FATHER'S DAY~~

I remember...uh...uh...come to think of it I remember nothing.
See my papa was no rolling stone.
45 minutes to an hour away my whole life.
Had more children and a wife.
2 story house with a nice yard and maybe even a dog type living.
I guess he never realized what was missing.

My brother and I always depended on our mother.
She was the light in the midst of the darkness that was you.
Providing us with all the things you didn't.
It wasn't just the love we missed.
But the fact that you never made an attempt that had us pissed.
No happy moments on which to reminisce.

Just the knowledge learned from the
school of single parents.
Super woman playing all parts:
mother, father, and disciplinarian.
Finally got the courage to let this
all out but you, you'll never read
this.
Cause after all these years if you
can't already see this you're worse
than I thought.
But you probably thought that it was
great that your child support was
hardly ever late.

I mean sure that's more than some
men do.
But real men know that child support
doesn't support a child the way a
father does.
Didn't turn me into the daddy's girl
I was supposed to be.
Instead I learned that some men
don’t care to guide their daughters
or raise their sons.
But on this fathers day I want to
say thank you.

You showed me what a father is by
being everything one is not.
And I thank you for that.
Thank you for being an excuse that I
will never make for any man in my
life.
I know the type of man I deserve and
he's the exact opposite of you.
And with that, all of this was just
to say,
Happy Father’s day,
Daddy.

Purposeless

Why do I feel alone with all these
people around?
Maybe it's me.
My life isn't going the way it
should be.
Don't have the things I want & it
seems I'll never get.
I'll never get there.
Why can't I get there?

Emptiness is all I feel.
Like the world is moving without me.
Never can catch up; never will catch
up.
Walk around with my head held up
Still feels like I'm looking down.
And Loneliness surrounds.
What will become of me?

I don't wanna feel this way forever.
Can't feel this way much longer.
Don't know how to fix it
But I don't wanna live like this,
So filled with,
Emptiness.

~~Thoughts~~

I wonder what would happen if I were
to just, drive off this bridge.
Let go of the wheel, drift over to
the side and then, fly right over
the edge.
Crash into the water below me let
the mouth of the sea swallow me
completely.
Maybe the reports would say,

"A young female lost control of
her vehicle and crashed into the
water below killing herself today.
The girl had hopes of being a
college graduate. How very tragic!"

Would anybody have a clue that my
death was no accident?
Is there someone out there that
knows the smile in my eyes is really
a smoke signal for pain?
Is there someone that can hear the
tremble in my steps, feel the
heaviness of my breath?
Somebody speak up!

Please don't lie to me!
Has anybody been paying attention
but you just failed to mention?
Didn't tell me that you saw through
me.
Through this facade & didn't try to
help me.
Didn't try to grab the wheel and
place me back on my path before I
got so lost in this forest that now
I can't even see the trees.

Or maybe you know me so well that
you know that I'll never take it to
that extent.
You know that I'm too afraid to be
such a disappointment.
To be such a failure to ever be the
reason that my body dies
Even though they already killed my
spirit.

Such a sad occasion to be stared at
and not be seen at the same time.
They pretend to pick me up only to
beat me further down.

They are in everything that's been
holding me down.
Taking turns clipping at my wings.
I do not soar, anymore.
So sometimes, my thoughts wander...

Cracks in the Foundation

These walls couldn't stand the test
of time.
The foundation was not strong
enough;
Structure was not sound.
Roof was not properly bound.
We have no reason or rhyme.
Can't understand how the walls could
not stand the test of time.
Generationally challenged
Habitual haters
Sins passed down
House full of traitors.
53 takes the crown pound for pound.

~~Murder at 53~~

I've been dead for a long time now.
You see they killed me a long while ago.
But even they didn't know how they murdered me.
Slaughtered involuntarily,
They all had a part in killing me.

Took my voice so I could no longer speak and that's when I started dying.
But death came quickly.
They stabbed me with their screams and beat me with their rolling eyes.
The looks of disgust were like upper cuts to the gut.
The sound of teeth sucking felt the same as a knife, Cutting.

"Nobody wants to hear that."
"I know that ain't hurt your feelings so stop crying and quit lying!"
They said my feelings were a lie and I had no reason to cry.

They let me know that it wasn't them
on who I could rely.
They took my voice away and now I
can't speak out loud.
I blame my mothers death for all my
tears.
Can't express my true feelings to
save my life.
Murdered, without a gun or knife.

How could they do this to me?
Why couldn't they just listen to me?
Why couldn't y'all just listen?

Hurricane

My heart feels like a storm is
raging in me
Ready to burst with destruction.
You disregard my feelings.
Now why should I care about yours?

A tornado twister is coming
My blood is ripping through my
veins.
Like waves surging violently through
the sea
A tsunami is on the way.

Alert! Alert! Alert!
You've been detected and now
identified.
Nothing can stop this storm.
I tried.

But you kept pushing and pushing me
to the side.
I've been hurt for the last time.
Look out,
There's a category 5 on the rise.

Blank pages remind me of me...

Part II: Lost

~~'06 Rage~~

AAAAAHHHHHHHH
AAAAAAAHHHHHHHHH
AAAAAAHHHHHHHHHH
AAAAAAHHHHHHHHHH
AAAAAAAHHHHHHHHH
AAAAAAAHHHHHHHHHHHHH
AAAAH AAAH AAAAH AAAH
AAAAAAAAAAAAAAAAAAAAAAAAAAA
AAAAAAAAAAAAAAAHHHHHHHHHHHH
HHHHHH AAAAAHHHHHHHHHHHHHH

If I could do this out loud
right now, I would.
Scream!

Run-On Reality

Caged in
Trapped
Tears fall
Constant
Y'all pretend
Everybody
I Lose
Always
No help
Ever
Nobody Listens
Still
No Words
Silent
I Speak
Never
My Spirit
Dying
Never Flying
Tired
From Trying
Pain
Consumes Me
Internally
Everything’s Fine

Outside
My Face
Smiles
My Body
Dances
My Words
Lie
My Soul
Cries
I Cry Everyday
All Alone On My Own Cause Nobody
Ever Wants To Listen For Real Y'all
Never Hear My Cries And I Need Help
But Y'all aren't Listening And I
Just Keep Crying Hoping One Day
Somebody Will Open Their Mouths And
Hear Me Help Me Tell Me Hug Me Love
Me Hold Me Show Me
Cause I Don't Know How To Stop
Crying The Pain Doesn't End
Just Like This Sentence Runs On
My Tears Running On The Curves Of My
Face Their Favorite Place Leave My
Cheeks Burning To Be Free Just Like
Me Just Like Me Can Anybody Hear Me
I'm Crying For Help Look At Me Just
Look At Me...

~~A Mess~~

This is what a mess looks like.
Pretty and perfect.
This is what a mess looks like.
On the inside she's hurting.
This is what a mess looks like.
She’s got it all together.
This is what a mess looks like.
Strength as light as a feather
This is what a mess looks like.
A big bright smile.
This is what a mess looks like.
It has looked this way for a while.
Lost and confused.
Broken and abused.
Ashamed and betrayed.
Lonely yet lovely.
Loving but still longing for love
Still longing for love.
A mess has no confidence yet looks
full of pride.
A mess self doubts and only goes
through happy bouts.
This is what a mess looks like.
A mess looks like...
A mess looks a lot like, Me.

Cover Up

A burst of laughter escaping her
mouth
Exposing her teeth, straight from
the braces she wore some time ago.
Her teeth, they fall into each other
perfectly with no gaps in between.
And when laughter comes and her lips
curl up from a smile as beautiful as
the sunrise,
Look into her eyes.

Her eyes
They light up like Christmas time.
As the wind begins to blow, listen
for the melody beneath it.
Watch as it blows its subtle breeze,
its music chiming through the trees.
Feel its voice against your skin,
like Gods hand placed on the
shoulder of your sin.
See her for who she really is.

For what is a smile with no voice?
What is laughter with no face?
What is wind with no breeze?

She is wind with no breeze.
There is no sunrise in her eyes if
you look deep inside.
She is a crooked smile, empty like
the spaces in between gapped teeth.

If you look closely enough you'll
see the curl of her lips is really a
quiver.
Her laugh, the misbeat of heart
Her rhythm is off.
There is no harmony in her melody.
What was once a beautiful symphony,
now a scratched CD
Skipping across the holes in her
heart, the spaces braces couldn't
fix.

Look her in the eyes and hear the
pain hiding inside.
Listen for the wind, and as it
dances across your skin, feel her
scream.
A smile with no voice, laughter with
no face, she is wind with no breeze.
Blowing trumpets of her agony,
but no one sees.

~~Confusion~~

I just can't be happy. And I don't know why...

Associates

I knew it.
I could always feel it.

As a child, as I grew
Maybe it'll get better.

Just a thought, still not a reality
But I knew it.
I could always feel it.

Like something wasn't right.
Like I didn't belong.
I could see it coming.

Here it is.
Burning inside of me.

A chilling fever, sweat on my skin
Reality sinking in, and I knew it.
I knew it.
I could always feel it.

Thoughts cloud my mind and fill my
heart.

When the day goes, the sound of
others voices no longer glows.
And I know...

I have no friends.
I still feel it.
A reality held deep within.

~~Single Epiphany~~

It sucks when you have so much to say but no one you can say it to. After almost 22 years I have no one I can talk to. That's the moment when you realize that in a world full of people you're all alone. I get it.

I put on a fake smile to hide the pain. Yet, I wish someone would look closely enough and see how broken I really am inside.

Reasons

I cry tears for you.
For the things we will never do.
For missing you.

I cry tears for missing you,
Missing you more than I could ever
express.
I cry tears for missing the way you
knew.

The way you knew I needed a kiss or
a hug,
I cry tears for the way I miss your
love.
Your love was like life, breathing
breath into my body.

Perfect like the pictures you didn't
like to take.
When the doctor said the words I
felt my heart break.
And I cry tears for you.

For the memories we were supposed to
share.

I cry tears for the pain I can hardly bear.
You were my air.

Haven't breathed right since you left.
And my heart no longer beats the same.
I will never be the same because what happened cannot change.

You died and I cry.
I cry tears for you.
For me,
For us.

For the things I'll never know.
The lessons never taught.
For the roads never traveled.

Mother and daughter
All ours plans,
Canceled.

~~Gone With the Wind~~

The wind blew my heart away.
Now I'm just staring at trees.
I just wanted to feel important.
I can't tell if anybody loves me.
Looked up and saw a heart in
the sky.

But the wind came and took it away.

A car just drove by
followed by another.

Mine sits still with me in it.
Nowhere for me to go,
So I look for hearts in the sky.
I love,
But never does the wind bring
it back.

Weight Gain

Been carrying this weight on my shoulders
But now the loads starting to get heavier,
My steps a little slower
And my back, my backs beginning to hunch over.

Like the posture of slaves who carry the burdens of the summer sun
The heat is becoming so unbearable that the sweat burns off my skin and I can no longer feel.
Where love was once rooted deep within, sorrow has now crept in.

Applying pressure to my bones now weak from worry.
I grow wearier everyday.
Trying to move forward but this proves too heavy.
I am stagnant.

Stuck in a time that I guess wasn't
meant to last but I can't seem to
get past.
I am still 12 years old.
Still a girl whose world will never
be the same.
The weight of the doctor's words
still heavy on my back,

Weigh so heavy on my brain that my
heart feels under attack.
21 years old but I'd give anything
to have the first 12 back.
All I want is my mama back.

Instead, I carry my broken spirit in
a sack, slung across my back.
And I don't know how much longer I
can bear it.

~~The Live Experience~~

She lives,

But only vicariously...

Who Am I

A question I ask myself often
Who I'm supposed to be is not really me.
Maybe I'm the tears wrapped up inside of me.
The ones tucked deep between the cavities of my chest,
Afraid to show themselves to the world...

No.

That can't be me; it's not supposed to be.

What if I'm the pain stuck in my bones?
Pain that puts a chokehold on my soul
So strong that I can barely make it to my next breath.

Wait.

That can't be right, can it?

I might still be the little girl I once was.

The little girl who heard the love
in her mother's eyes,
Or maybe it's my ears that became
blind.

Who am I?

Your guess is as
good as mine.

~~Love Name~~

A simple word that brought so much joy
A word that I too often took for granted
With so much more meaning than one could imagine.
Not a word but a nickname.

One that I held proudly,
But I haven't heard it in a while.
9 years to be exact.
The last thing you said to me as a matter of fact,
Not a nickname but a love name.

And I came running when I heard my name called
In the most beautifully beautiful voice ever sent to ring in my ears.
Took me to a place of true happiness and peace.
A place that I have yet to find since then

But when I close my eyes I am taken home again.
The sweet sound of your voice fills my mind
Your heart hugs mine,
And I smile when I hear it.

Not a word but a nickname.
Not a nickname but a love name.
My mother called me Pumpkin.
And I loved that name.

Sunshine

Flowers are beautiful, just like my
mother was.
Somehow they seem to lose color,
like I lost my mother.

Flowers grow, as do I.
They lose pedals; I think I'm losing
my mind.

Flowers blow with the wind, free
like I want to be.
Flowers don't always bloom,
But somewhere underneath the gloom
There's always,
SUNSHINE.

I won't say I'm looking, but I do wish I could find it...

Part III: Searching

~~Second Epiphany~~

You may think you have no life.
But what a sad confirmation when
others show you this to be true.
- Epiphany # 2

Tears From the Sky

Laying here on my bed I have so many
thoughts in my head.
I can hear the faint sounds of
roommate's voices floating through
the wall like a ghost from a dream.
I can hear rain falling from the
sky, the wind sighing through it,
Giving a voice to Gods' cries.

I close my eyes and picture what
Heaven looks like.
A place where everyone is alive and
no one ever dies
Where there are no shadows hiding
from the sun
And the moon lights up the entire
night so the sky is always blue.

Nobody runs from the rain.
Instead, they dance in its beauty
then tilt their heads back to catch
the drops on their tongues.

A place where you roll with the
thunder, and pray for lighting to
strike so that you can feel the God
in you.

I open my eyes still lying on my
bed,
Same thoughts in my head.
My roommate's are still talking.
God is still crying.
And so am I.

Ready…Or Not

I do a good job of hiding myself.
But one day this game will be over
And I'll find me somewhere
Right now all I know is tears.

See they remain constant
Constantly breaching the gates of my tear ducts
Then running swiftly down my face
They always manage to escape my closed eyelids.

I cry in the shower so that they will blend in.
A perfect hiding place,
Stopping only for a moment to reach my bedroom.
Such a safe place enclosed by these four walls.
Maybe one day I can escape as my tears do.
Breaking down these walls that keep me caged in,
Unleashing this woman within.

But the problem is,
I don't know who she is.

She's been hiding for so long, I'm
not sure I can sing her song.
One day, this game will end.
I just hope that I am ready to begin
again.

Hope

One day I'll be done with this.
One day I'll be all done with this.
One day I'll be over this.
One day I'll gain control of this.
One day I'll be free of this.
One day I'll make sense of this.
One day...

~~Funny Money~~

I wanted my bed to be comfortable so
I bought satin sheets and an
expensive comforter set.

I wanted a place to call home so I'm
renting a house.

I wanted to look good walking down
the street so I bought new clothes.

I wanted to go places at my own free
will so I bought a car.

I wanted to make good grades in my
classes so I bought all of my books.

I wanted to keep the sun out of my
eyes so I bought some fake aviator
glasses.

I wanted a lifetime with my mother
but you can't buy time.

What a game of deception I've
played.

Making my life look full with all the money I paid...

...I should've kept the receipts.

Ugly Beautiful

The ugly is hiding in my beautiful.
All this time
I guess I should've noticed
something unusual.
Caused so much pain,
Like a hangnail in a cuticle.

How long has this ugly been in my
beautiful?
Undetected.
Never showing its true self
I thought all feelings were mutual
Ended up letting ugly manipulate
this beautiful.
My beautiful.

Your ugly was masked
And now finally unveiled I see.
The ugly, yet you still claim to be
that beauty.
Praising me and thanking me for
being me.
Words can be blinding.
But now my vision is free.

You have allowed me to see
That you are the ugly hiding inside my beauty
Replacing my yellows with black and my greens with blue.

Trying to fill my light with darkness
Want me to be ugly like you.
But I see right through you like a transparency.
So you won't stop me from being beautifully me.

~~About Time~~

Some people just don't understand
how deep certain things run with me.
I am no longer looking to those
people for understanding.
Taking a step in a different
[better] direction.
Better for me that is.
I've been talking it for a
while...now it's time for me to live
[love] it!

Love Undefined

Never had that love.
Can't say what it feels like.
Not sure what it even looks like.

Like it could literally walk right past me
Recognition not given.
Never knew that love thing.

Nah, I came up broken.
And now I'm just hopin’
I'm hopin’ I can fix it.

Learn how to fix me.
There's love somewhere lost within me.
Maybe. Irrevocably. Broken.

But I'm hopin’
I'm hopin’ I can fix me.
Maybe Too late,
Try anyway.
Try love anyway...

WILDERNESS

Try love anyway   Try love anyway
Try love anyway   Try love   Try love Try love anyway
Try love anyway   Try love   Try love anyway
Try love anyway   Try   Try love anyway

Try love anyway   Try love anyway

Try love anyway   Try love anyway

Try love anyway   Try love anyway

Try love anyway

Try

~~3a.m. Unclosed Thoughts~~

Tonight my head hurts and I don't know why. But if I was to die and it be from the same cause as my mother's death [aneurysm], please don't judge the poems in this journal. Most were written in a time before I knew God loved me. But at the same time, they are all a true look into my feelings throughout my life.

To my family, I love you. Even through all the dysfunction. Please pray, work, build, and grow together. All I ever truly wanted was peace within my family, thus peace within myself.

Love,

Prayer Poems

One day I'll write a really happy
poem.
Thus far this journal is filled with
depression.
But one day, and obviously not
today, I'll have something really
joyful to say.
In Jesus name I pray.
Amen

Lord,
Since you know my heart,
Can you please send someone who
knows it's been ripped apart?
Maybe then I won't have to pretend.
Amen

Dear God,
I'm trying to stay positive but it's
hard when life feels so negative.
Maybe I'm just missing all the
good...However I don't believe so.
Jesus loves me, this I know.
Is there anybody else?
Well, make me believe so.
Amen

I Wonder

I wonder what it feels like to fly.
Just to soar through the sky so high
Flapping your wings against the wind
Then gliding across the sunrise into the sunset
From dusk 'til dawn, not stopping until all your worries are gone.

I wonder what it feels like to be so close to God.
So close to the heavens as if it's just beyond the next cloud
To escape this world so loud and break away from the crowd.

I wonder what it feels like to be free.
To move as quiet and calmly as the sea
Wave my wings through the breeze.

I wonder what it feels like to dream.
Close my eyes and drift to a place so peaceful and serene.

Feel the presence of God wrapped around me
Just like when my mother used to hold me.
Yeah I wonder.

I wonder what it feels like to be beautiful.
Not fine, but beautiful
Like true love is beautiful isn't it?

I wonder if that's real or, maybe if I'm really real.
I wonder if time really does heal all wounds.
I'm still bleeding slow from all those years ago.

I wonder.
I wonder when it's my time to go.

I wonder what it's like to be a rainbow.
To let all of your true colors show
To shine bright for all of the world to know.

I wonder if I jump high enough could
I fly?
Just once I wanna soar through the
sky.

Queens & Kings

Realize that you were born on this earth by no choice of your own.

But you can choose whether or not you claim your rightful place on your throne.

~~Self Discovery in America [Obama '08]~~

We cast spells like Scripps
Killing off the disease that you
spread like beds
No longer hiding under covers
We uncovered the truth

Truthfully we been considered evil
like Rosemary's baby
Trying to reach benevolence using
malevolent powers
See we've been getting done wrong
for so long
Tired of the same sad song

We steal we kill
We are walking breathing destruction
Thriving off of others
misfortunes...
Or so they say.

They who don't understand its power
or its purpose
Spitting curses at us like monkeys
in a 3-ring circus.

So we cut our emotional ties leaving
only the scars behind.

We are the dark arts not mentioned
in Harry Potter.
We are Jacob Lawrence, Langston
Hughes,
Zora Neale Hurston writing our way
through the New Renaissance.

We are Sidney Poitier, Ruby Dee,
We are Denzel Washington no longer
waiting on our Glory
We're rewriting our story and to God
be the glory.

We are powerful beyond measure.
With no fear
We are not afraid
There's nothing to prove to you.

We steal our dreams back, Black.
We kill your ability to block our
shine back, Black.

We are walking breathing destruction
thriving off the fire burning from

our own misfortunes in order to
reclaim our futures.

Place a hex around your necks
Yeah now you know how tight that
noose felt.

So tight that your eyes bulge out of
your head
Leaving you with no choice but to
see how bright our dark skin glow,
Even in the dead of the night while
we perform our “rituals”

Cause you know habits are habitual.
And this,
This is personal.
You may even say it’s tragic.
But this,
This is Black Magic.

Journey to My Dream (After Kanye)

You ever wonder what it all really means?
You wonder if you'll ever find your dreams?

So close yet so far it seems I'll never reach my destination
To want something so bad you feel like you can't function.

Wanting to shine like the sun
Dreaming on clouds, wishing on stars.

Feeling like a fool, so close yet so far it seems,
I'll never reach my dreams.
Can't seem to figure out what it all means.

Maybe its not meant to be
But that's the only place I see me being

Human beings can’t understand my
desire.

It’s like my soul is on fire
And as the flames start to consume
my heart
I pray for the rain to start.

Extinguish this burning blaze,
Leaving nothing but a smoky haze.

And when the clouds part and the sun
shines through, I will shine too.
I realize that real lies don’t make
it any more true.

You ever wonder what it all really
means?
You wonder if you’ll ever find your
dreams?

~~Relapse~~

For a minute there I had myself
fooled.
Thought I was done with my old ways.
But that only lasted a few days.
Then I was back.
And now, I am back.

Back at this place I can't seem to
erase.
First came the aggravation, then the
frustration, then more aggravation,
then anger, then rage!
Rage rushed through me like a heat
wave.

My whole body felt of fire.
My insides were burning.
And before I knew it...BOOM!
I exploded like a suicide bomb in
Baghdad.

My path of destruction catching
everything ablaze,
How swiftly my progress incinerates.

Yesterday I relapsed back to my not so old ways.
And now here I am again.
Beating myself up for what I can't take back.
I'm so stupid, I always over react.

AGGRAVATION

FRUSTRATION

AGGRAVATION

ANGER

RAGE

SADNESS

STUPIDITY

CONFUSION

REGRET

SELF HATE

REPEAT...

March 3: Unequivocal

What do you get when you mix the sun and the moon?
When your odd meets your even and even the odd makes sense.

But sense don't sell for cents.
Gotta have dollars to make change
And people expect you to change your clothes but not your mind.

They say a mind is a terrible thing to waste
But people have been minding mine for so long they must've lost theirs.

Be of sound mind and body.
My body may grow weary but my mind is made up like faces.
My mind is made up like faces.

I've laid the foundation
Brushed Sephora on my aura so you could feel the beauty around me
Still you look right past me.

Misjudged me.
And they said that was God's job.

But you didn't care to ask
My even equaled your odd
You thought my presence wasn't worth your time spent.

But I was ready to spend way more than cents.
Cause to me it made sense.
But you misunderstood.
Thought I was trying to mix the sun and the moon.

What a mistake I would have made.
No one wants to see the stars at noon.

I only changed my mind,
Or better yet followed my heart.
But I know, I know.
You don't care about that part.

~~Direction~~

Wisdom from The Elder...

Nobody, but nobody, can make it out here alone – Maya Angelou

Dreaming to Wake Up

And God said wake up.
Clear as Day, I heard him say,
Wake Up!

Tessie you're gonna have to wake up.
I've been trying to answer when you call
Sending you signs and letting my blessings fall
but I'm not sure if you really want it all.
You prayed for it, but first you must prepare for it.

You're gonna have to wake up my child.
My child of God
Meaning I am your father and you do as you're told.
No more putting your blessing on hold.
No amount of pressure should make you fold.

You're gonna have to wake up girl.
You're a grown woman now
No more child's play.
It's time to do this Gods way.
Listen carefully, follow these instructions and do as I say,

1. Pray:
Without ceasing and with all your heart, pray.
Yeah I know, you've been doing this everyday
But sometimes it seems that it's just a routine.
Do you really believe?

2. Believe:
Tessie, I need you to believe.
Not only in me but also in you.
You were fearfully and wonderfully made by my hands. There is purpose in you; seeds planted by me. Believe in yourself.
Confidence is key, trust me.

3. Trust:
I have never left your side.

I know I've done some things you
don't understand.
I know it feels like you've been
stuck in this unfamiliar land for
far too long
But I promise you I have a plan.
Are you following?

4. Follow:
Follow, but only me.
It is I who will light your path
leading to your destiny
But only if you stay with me.
And I'm sorry but no, everyone can't
go.
Some will have to stay behind.
Understand that they were not built
for your journey.
Your future does not depend on
theirs so please, let go of their
hands; stop grabbing at their
shirts.
I have something greater.
I know, I know, letting go hurts.

But I promise you; if you do these things your treasure will be revealed
And all pain will be healed.
You were not meant to live in the wild.

Now wake up my child.
For your response will determine your results.
Open your eyes and see that it is the start of a new day.
And you must
Follow,
Believe,
Trust, and
Pray.

Lord, I've been afraid of my greatness…

Part IV: Home

Recalculating Route

If life is a journey,

God is the GPS...

~~War, Peace~~

Where there is war there can also be found peace,
For nothing can exist without its opposite.
War an antonym for peace or peace for war
There are such things as peaceful wars.

Still we can't have both
No way to coexist without contradict
1989-2015 a perfect example of this.
1989, I was born during a hurricane.

The war outside of wind and trees
and all the helpless debris
And me, a newborn baby
There was peace in my eyes and even in my cries while the war raged on outside.

"We were so scared. We had no idea how we were going to warm your bottles." My mama once said.

Winds howled tossing the outside
like a rag doll.
Then Boom!
The pine tree snapped,
The roof cracked
But in the hallway our faith never
collapsed...

In 2001 my mother died.
The war on terror reigned for 12
years before the enemy troops
started to retreat.
Still a few left but they too will
soon face defeat.

Selfish Love

I took some time for myself.
I had to distance myself.
I love everybody.
But I had to care about myself.

~~Alive~~

The past is an illusion
The future is a fantasy
The present is me
Because in this moment I Be...

Forgiveness

Before my grandmother passed
Before the Alzheimer's stole what
was left of her memory, we had a
conversation.

She was lying in bed and she invited
me to lay with her.
"Get in" she said.
"Come on and get under the cover
with grandma"
So I climbed in.
Wrapped myself underneath the sheets
and snuggled up close to my granny.

It felt like old times there.
Like when I would have a tummy ache
and she'd rub my belly and rock me
to sleep there.
"Now go ahead and go to sleep next
to grandma," she said.
But instead,

I said grandma there's some things I need to say.
Some things I need to get off my chest.
Cause I know the day is near where although you'll still be able to listen you might not be able to really hear.

And there are some things I need to say to you.
There's some air I need to clear.
Grandma don't fall asleep just yet.
As my face grew wet with tears pouring from my eyes,
"Talk" she said.

Grandma, I am sorry.
Sorry for every time I disrespected you.
For every time I yelled at you.
Rolled my eyes at you.
Slammed doors in your house.
Told you to leave me alone when you were just trying to help.

I was a stupid girl,
Lost and confused.
I lost my mother and at times I took my sadness out on you.
You, a mother, who lost her daughter too.
And then was tasked with the job of raising hers too.

I should've been more loving toward you.
I should've done more hugging and less huffing,
more kissing and less hissing
and grandma I am sorry.
It's too late now and I can't go back.
Believe me I would if I could.
Would go back and be everything a granddaughter should.

Would appreciate you while your brain still understood.
For every doctors appointment you drove me to,
For every plate you made me,
For every day you gave me.

Every prayer you prayed me.
Every day you raised me.
Grandma, You saved me.

And I am sorry for not always
treating you like I should.
I would go back if I could.
But I can't.
So I am here,
Lying in bed,
Snuggled under the sheets with you.
Hoping that this message gets
through before the Alzheimer's takes
what's left of you.

"Okay" she said.
And she rubbed my head.

Before my grandmother passed,
Before the Alzheimer's stole what
was left of her memory.
We had a conversation.

~~Choose Freedom [4a.m. Revelation]~~

You owe yourself freedom.
Waiting on some to apologize for
what they did to you or didn't do
for you will have you bound forever.

Let it go...and while you're at it,
forgive yourself too...
You owe yourself freedom.
Wake up free.

10 Finally, be strong in the Lord
and in the strength of his might.
11 Put on the whole armor of God,
that you may be able to stand
against the schemes of
the devil. - Ephesians 6:10-11

Love Defined [After Forgiveness & Freedom]

Me and my father ain't that close.
We talk on the phone every once in a while
And I know that might be better than most but still we ain't that close.

We've never been
And I'm grown now so I guess I can take some of the blame.
I know his birthday and I don't call or say Happy Father's Day
No text just to say, hey.
I mean, me and him just ain't that close

I ain't daddy's girl and I really don't care to be.
I ain't mad at him but sometimes I do wonder why he wasn't there for me.

Miss me with the financially I'm talking bout daddily.

Yeah I said daddily!
Hope he don't be mad at me if he sees this, or hears this, or read this
Hope he don't take it as a diss.

We ain't that close
It's the truth.
I write to get free so I gotta speak my peace.
When my mama died I grieved and you weren't there for me

I mean I spent a night two.
Two nights under a roof with you but was still so far from you.

But this ain't a diss
I'm not trying to get at you.
Don't think I'm attacking you.
I write so I can get free so I gotta speak my peace
And right now I'm in disbelief
My grandma just died and she finished raising me when you didn't.

She wiped the tears from my eyes
that you weren't even there to see
So as I'm thinking of her I got a
slight image of you.
But this poem aint even really about
you as much as it is me.
Me and my father ain't that close
and that's cool
I'm sure he's a good dude, people
really seem to like him

And me, I turned out to be awesomely
amazing excellent Crown Me Queen
Tessie.
Strong, independent, God fearing,
self loving, dream chaser, goal
digger, won't give up or give in,
never break no matter how far she
been bent...

Somehow it all makes sense,
My crown fits regardless.
Me and my father ain't that close
But this ain't about that.
I'm loved enough without that.
God My Father taught me all that.

~~Today I Became A Bird~~

Not just a walk across the stage,
More of a flying out of a cage
Not just a comma and three letters behind my name.

This here is different...Beyond a ritual
No this is spiritual.
A God gifted miracle.

So much division subtracted from my equation,
M.B.A.
This here Marvelous celebration of a graduation,
I made it.

But I don't really have the words to explain it.
Don’t really know how I can express it.
It’s like, today I became a bird.

No more wondering what it’s like to fly.

I gained a new perspective.
So many years all I did was cry
wishing I could soar through the
sky.

And today I became a bird.
I graduated and though I've
accomplished this before.
This time it means so much more.

This time I did for me.
This time I did it caring about
myself,
Loving myself,
And not being so critical of myself.

This time, I gave myself time to
find myself.
And I didn't let others define
myself.

Who knew I had wings all along...

Something Really Joyful

No More Faking
I used to be really good at
pretending I was happy...Now I'm
just really happy!
#WhatJoyFeelsLike

Sappy
I'm so happy that things make me sad.
Or that I can look at a picture or video of someone else's joy and feel my emotions flow through me so freely,
slow enough for me to appreciate its beauty.
#GodChangedMyHeart

~~The Banjo Lesson~~

The Banjo Lesson hanging on the wall
the first thing I see, a reminder
for me
of this place of peace
In this space for me.

Not a mansion but it's big enough
for me.
Big enough for me to grow into.
Big enough for me to add all my
clutter to,
But small enough for me to
appreciate this space.
This place of peace I have earned.

Growing up I learned how to value
that precious entity.
15 people and 3 bedrooms doesn't
leave a lot of room.
Creates a lot of noise.
Plenty things to do,
Always somebody to talk or listen to
Plenty fights,
Plenty "imma tell my mama on you."

Plenty sleepless nights,
Plenty prayers to God to make it
alright.
Plenty of grandmas home cooked meals
Fried chicken, mac and cheese, &
collard greens.

The light hardwood we discovered
hiding under the dark navy blue
carpet floor.
We had a bright red front door that
people were always welcome to walk
through,
and stay as long as they need to.
A squeaky screen that never quite
closed right,
that we never bothered locking at
night.

That house on the block that
everybody would flock to.
Minimal square footage with an
abundance of people at all times.
The dining room served double duty
for Dominos and Pity Pat

The Banjo Lesson hanging on the
wall,
My mother's favorite painting and
the first thing I use to see
Now, a reminder of how it use to be.
Inspiring to not have to go back to
still carry it with me.
There is no other art on my wall
No other pictures I need to see.
My mother's Banjo Lesson

Wilderness

I was only 12 years old when my mom
died and I entered
this wilderness.
I cried and I cried
I tried and I tried but I couldn't
get out of,
this wilderness.

Seasons changed.
Falls to winters
not a leaf left to leave,
Trees empty.

Everything leaving but me.
Everything leaving me,
Lost, in this wilderness.

Springs came,
Birds sang,
Flowers sprang.

Everything grew but me
Everything growing, but me.
Lifeless, in this wilderness.

So small I couldn’t see the forest
nor the trees,
Nobody could find me.
Lost, in this wilderness.

Everything green, including me,
with envy.
Mad cause it seemed everybody had
everything but me.
Camouflaged they couldn’t see me.

Couldn’t see me screaming, crying,
fighting, bleeding.
Couldn’t see me needing.
Needing someone to find me.

I waited and waited but I didn’t
leave a track.
I prayed and I prayed but it didn’t
bring my mama back.

Stop that.

I wanna get out of here.
Gotta back track.

How did I get here in this
wilderness?

Been here for over a decade too
long.
I need to find my way home.

Back track.

How did I get here?
What was the point of **ENTRY**?

Loss.

Loss led me to **LOST**.

All this time spent **SEARCHING**.
Who do I need to find?

God.

God will lead me to me.
To the perfect place of peace He
designed for me.

Where is He?

He is within me.

Has He been here the whole time?

Yes.

He's shown himself many times but
somchow I still remained blind.
He was my teachers and my preachers,
My mother and my father,
My strength like no other.
Who else could've kept me?

So this whole time God was keeping
me?

Keeping me through the hurt, the
depression, the anger, and the pain.
So he's the one who put the pen in
hand at 13 and told me to write
myself free or else suicidal
thoughts might get the best of me?
Through this, wilderness
He's been, carrying me?

Yes.

And now he wants to give his best to
me.
No more making excuses and settling
for less.
This is called blessed.

This is what a blessing looks like.

Feels like?

Feels like refreshed.
Feels like Freedom.

Freedom.
I can longer see the forest cause I
made it through the trees.
Through the mud and the dirt.
Made it past all the hurt.
Through the mistakes I had to wait,
As He built my faith.

When I was a child, I found myself
in the wild.
And now, I FOUND myself in the wild.
Forced in, but I walked out.
I made it out.
No more need to back track.
God said, I get my life back.

Welcome **HOME**...

Made in the USA
Columbia, SC
25 January 2022

54801695R00069